Kid's
Guide
To Organizing

A Kid's Guide to Organizing
Jarrett G. Carter
Janae J. Carter
Jolene T. Carter

ISBN- 0-9669899-8-8

Library of Congress Number-2002106828

Published by Jehonadah Communications
Post Office Box 712
Long Island, New York 11553-0712

SAN #254-1963

Quantity Discounts Available. Email- Info@momtime.net

Cover & book design:
Jehonadah Communications
P.O. Box 712
Long Island, New York 11553-0712
United States of America

The information in this book is true and complete to the best of our knowledge. It is offered without guarantee on the part of the author or publisher. The authors and publisher disclaim all liability in connection with the use of this book.

Website-www.momtime.net

The following trademarks appear throughout this book :Microsoft WORD, PC Fonts and Microsoft Clip Art.

A Kid's Guide To Organizing

By
Jarrett G. Carter
Janae J. Carter
Jolene T. Carter

Dedication

Dedicated to our friend-Brandon Locke,
who gave us the idea for writing this book.
Thanks Brandon.

Here it is!

Thanks So Much!

Many thanks to our dad and mom, who helped us to be diligent when writing this book. Thank you for believing in us and for all your time editing and typesetting our work. Also thank you for not changing what we really wanted to say. We love you!

"Cleaning your room can be fun. It's like searching for buried treasure"

The Way This Book Was Written

We, Janae and Jarrett wrote different chapters. Jolene helped us write the tips. All of us answered the questions. We hope you enjoy reading and become more organized. We had fun writing this book and we learned a lot in the process.

"Rushing always causes disorder. So stop and take the time to figure out why you're always rushing. Take the time to organize yourself."

A Kid's Guide To Organizing

Part One

Introduction
Why a Kid's Guide To Organizing
Page 15

Chapter One
Making the Most Of Your Day
Learn how to set a schedule and make your day more productive
Page 17

Chapter Two
Clean Your Room
Learn to keep your room clean even with messy siblings.
Page 24

Chapter Three
Finding A Place For Everything
Learn how to organize your room and find lost items.
Page 29

Part Two

Part Three

Part Four

Practical Work Sheets To Help You Become More Organized

Fun Worksheets

Part One

Getting Organized!

"Do it first the right way or your parents will come along and do it the wrong way. In other words clean up your room before your parents do it for you."

Why An Organizing Book Just For Kids?

We decided to write an organizing book for kids for two reasons because:

<u>One</u>
Now-a-days adult organizing books are not practical enough for kids. Kids cannot understand them yet kids, just like adults, need to be organized. When our friend Brandon Locke talked to us about not being able to find an organizing book for kids we, thought we should write one. Some adults think kids do not care about organizing, but we really do!

<u>Two</u>
We believe that it shouldn't be just be the parent's responsibility to organize the house. We believe that families should work together and organizing is a good place to start.

"When your mom wants to spend quality time with you while she's holding a mop and pail, beware!"

Chapter One

Making the Most Out Of Your Day!

School days tend to feel like short days because of one thing-homework and schoolwork. It's like you get no time to yourself to do the things you really want to do.

You need to know how get time for yourself and for everything else. That's why you should set a schedule. How do you do that? It's easy.

First fill in the chart on Worksheet E-1, the Perfect Day Worksheet. Write down how you want to spend your day. Start in the morning when you first get up and record everything until bedtime. Include television and play time. This would be your perfect day, do not think about what your parents or teachers would say about it. This writing exercise is just for you to see not to get your parents' approval.

Remember to include the things you have to do like schoolwork and chores. Be realistic when you make up your perfect day chart. It's not fair to think you can spend your whole day playing because your day would not really be productive.

I like my days to be productive. Being productive to me means getting as much done as possible during the day. For instance, when I started writing this book I had to put writing time into my day even though sometimes I wanted just to have free time. But since I had a goal, I just kept writing. I felt good when I finally finished the book. I had achieved my goal. Goals are important.

Goals are important because they help you plan your day. A goal is something you would like to do some day. Isn't there something you want to accomplish? Make it a goal and you can do it! Just give yourself a date you want to accomplish your goal. Then plan to make it happen.

The important thing is that every goal needs a plan if you really want to see it happen. Our mom says a goal without a plan is a fantasy because it will never happen.

See Worksheets G and H-1 which will show you how to write a goal. We call it our goal planning sheets.

All goals must be completed by a certain time. Goals are big things you have to break into little steps in order to get it done. Goals will help you in your everyday planning because you can schedule the steps. For instance, I put writing everyday into my schedule because my goal was to get writing published. Writing daily is a small step to my bigger goal of finishing a book.

So you can see goals and daily planning are related. Like I said before, you need to know where all your time is going. You do this by looking at your day. Once you've written down what a perfect day is for you, look at it closely. Remember to fill in the chart thoroughly including television and play time. Write down what you actually do-- not what you wish you had done. This will help you to see where all your time is going. It may surprise you.

Now do Worksheet F which will show you how you really spend your time. Can you see where you might make changes? I bet you can. This is a fun thing to do with your friends, parents or brothers and sisters. Everyone can share how to make your actual day more like your perfect day.

You might also want to do this for a typical a weekend. You may also record your day in fifteen minute intervals to see where all your time is going. This is kind of hard to do it, but if you do it with some one else it is easier. Your parents might like to do this with you. They may even want to try it themselves.

When you are comparing both time charts, make adjustments. You may want to save most of your playtime for the weekend. That's how I adjusted my schedule after I compared my time charts. After this you will have the beginnings of a more productive day. You just need to work on your daily schedule.

Everyone needs a To-Do list. Some kids use a Palm Pilot or some sort of electronic organizer to record their schedule. Even if you do not have one of these devices, you can use pen and paper to write down the things you need to get done. You can also photocopy Worksheet K in Part Five of this book. Your parents can also buy a school organizer for you. I prefer the adult ones because the kid organizers usually only account for school time.

Your To-Do list will really help you to be organized. I use numbers to indicate if you really need to do something. The greater the number the more important it is to get done that day. Try it. I only schedule a few important things a day. See Worksheet K to see what I mean.

Sleep is also very important. So do not plan too much in a day. You should go to bed early. I'm sure you have heard Benjamin Franklin said "Early to bed early to rise makes a man healthy, wealthy and wise."

In other words you will be able to get up earlier if you go to bed earlier. That means less of a rush in the morning which means less stress. I know when I go to bed very late, I find it hard to get up in the morning. Even though I may be having fun at night I sometimes force myself to go to bed because I know I will regret going to bed late the next morning.

It's okay to relax this rule sometimes like on Friday nights I stay up late because I can sleep in on Saturday. Just keep in mind that on average people say children should get at least ten hours of sleep every night.

Besides sleep, it is most important that I do three things for myself everyday. You should do something special for yourself everyday too! I always pray, read my Bible, and listen to God. To be honest I don't do these things everyday but I really do try to do them everyday. You may have special devotional books you like to read, or maybe you talk to your parents. The important thing is you do something to build yourself up. Also I try to exercise everyday but when I am running around a lot I count that as exercise for the day. You should try to work on your goals and things that build you up everyday too.

Remember that goals are very important. Goals help us to see pass today and into tomorrow. After all, if I didn't know how to make goals you wouldn't be reading this book.

"It's time to clean your room when your baby sister can get on the top bunk without climbing the ladder."

Chapter Two

Clean Your Room!

Your room would probably be neater if you didn't have messy siblings. So, here are two things you can do. 1 - Beg your parents to make your siblings live in the basement or garage. 2 -Cooperate with your siblings.

Well, let's focus on solution number two for now. Cooperate. Cooperate basically means to work together on one accord. This method takes a bit of patience.

First keep a record of what she drops and how many times she drops it. At this point do not tell her what you are doing. Just keep records for a few days. Then go and talk with her after you have collected your data. Be certain you go with the right attitude. Be ready to really help her- do not criticize her for being messy. Your data should be used to come up with a solution. It should help you both figure out why things keep ending up on the floor. Attitude is everything here!

Share your list with your sister. Ask her if she has a place for the things that keep ending up on the floor. If she has a place and she is just rushing around all the time suggest she put "organize your room" time in her daily schedule.

Convincing her to change her schedule may be difficult. She might not want to clean everyday, but if you can convince her to try it for just two weeks you're in a good position. Since she will see the result of a neater room after picking up daily, she may really want to cooperate with you. No one likes a sloppy room not even messy people.

Once she agrees you can both clean the room together. This will also get her attention. As she sees that you want to cooperate with her too, she will cooperate with you. You can form the clean-your-room team. Throw out what you do not need. Get a big trash bag and try to throw out as many things as possible. Throw out old and broken toys. Games are also useless if you are missing pieces.

Make a place for the things she keeps dropping on the floor. I think you should be fair in room space. If she needs more room give it to her. I am not saying give her all space but try to think of ways to compromise. Knowing how to compromise is one lesson everyone has to learn sooner or later. Why not start now?

Does she have a place for the things she keeps dropping on the floor? If not, help her find a place to put things. Hang things on the wall. Store them in boxes in the closet. Be creative. I'm sure you can find ways to find space. We kids are pretty good at finding hidden space.

Once your room is clean and organized, you can work on keeping it that way with your sister. You can make room rules which you both agree to keep. Perhaps, you can make a room contract. In the contract you can both agree to do certain things to keep the room clean. Sign it in front of your parents.

If none of these suggestions work then there's always the garage or basement.

"When you come to your desk you should come with a smile not a pile. Don't just throw stuff on your desk."

Chapter Three

Organizing Your Stuff !

Kids can have lots of stuff so I'm going to help you find a place to put it. First things first, your mom or dad will probably tell you to do is throw away or give away your stuff. Do it!

You should volunteer to give your stuff away because if you don't your parents will throw away something that is valuable to you. It's unfortunate, but I think most parents don't remember how it was to be a kid. They don't know the difference between junk and valuable treasure.

We really cannot expect them to know what to keep and what to throw out. Since we know we should be the ones to do it. Got it! Sometimes when we don't clean or organize our stuff our mom throws out some of our best things. So don't let this happen to you.

Rule number one of organizing do it first the right way or else your parents will come along and do it the wrong way. Are you ready to do it the right way? Good.

So get three large trash bags. Label each bag.

"Keep it."

"Trash it."

"Give it."

If you want to keep it, put it in the keep it bag. You should only keep something, if you honestly use it or treasure in some special way. I would never give away my dolls just because they are taking up space in my room. Instead, I just find a spot for them. There are other things we need to throw away like old school projects, old games and broken toys. You know what I mean. You can't use it, so throw it out.

Anything you choose to keep you should have a particular place for it already. The things in the keep it bag will be put in their proper place. I keep some special books and toys even though I do not play with them; however, I store them in a special place so they are not in the way.

The reason you have the "Keep It" bag is so you do not stop cleaning to put it away. After you finish cleaning, then you put your "Keep It" bag stuff away. You can go faster cleaning and organizing, if you just put it in a bag for now. Make time to put it in its proper place later.

If you want to throw it away put it in the "Trash It" bag. Remember to throw out broken toys and games with missing pieces and old papers. Sometimes we need to give ourselves that little nudge to throw things out. You might feel like you are really losing something important. I try to think of the last time I used it. I have learned, if I have not used something in a long time I probably won't miss it.

I hold onto one or two special things and give away the rest. I like the "Give It" bag because that's where I put things I will give away. Sometimes I find it is easier to give things away instead of throwing things away. Don't you? I give my old baby toys to friends at church and babies who visit our family. A lot of babies visit our family so we don't have many baby toys left.

After you put things the "Trash It" bag, put it in the garbage before you change your mind. Please do not throw out family members stuff. They have to do throw out their own things. Look how hard it is for you to do it. Imagine how they would feel if you threw their treasures out.

BOOKS

We have a lot of books around our house. We put our books in categories so we can find them. You can put all story books, chapter books and classics in different sections. Remember to give away your toddler or board books when you outgrow them. It's okay to save one or two special board books just in case you want to read them when no one's around. I won't tell anyone.

We have a library book box in our house. We put our library books in it so we do not lose them. We are only allowed to in read our books in room where the library box is located. Sometimes I go other places in the house anyway, but I try to remember to put the books back in the library box when I am finished reading. I have my own personal library box too to help me remember to return the books.

You can make a library box in your own room if you like. You can paint or decorate your own box. An old computer box makes a great family library box. I like to use a crate for my personal library books because I can carry the crate from room-to-room with me. Crates are great to put personal stuff in you want to take from room-to-room with you.

Clothes

You probably already know to sort your clothes. You know what I mean, you put your pants in one draw and your shorts in the other. Some kids like to do it this way. Sometimes its nice to put whole outfits together instead of separating each item of clothing. This saves you searching time and you don't have to convince your parents that what you're wearing really matches.

Use your closet space first. Hang up as many clothes as possible. Be careful not to crowd your closet, to the point where you have so many clothes that you cannot find things in your closet. Put your play clothes where it's easier to get to them. Separate any clothing that is too small for you especially when the seasons change and your mom or dad stores your clothes for the next season. You can put a bag in your closet for clothing that is too little for you. You can give it to your mom or dad when they are giving away old clothes or passing them down to your brother or sister.

Toys

You can put your games in a large plastic container. We like to store our toys and games in categories using an old dresser. Plastic see-through shoe boxes also make good containers for toys.

Paper and Art Projects

Most of these things you will probably give to your mom or dad. If you have a really special project you can put it on your wall or the refrigerator. You may want to get an arts and craft box. You may also ask your mom or dad to buy you an under-the-bed storage box so you can easily store your stuff. Tell them it will help keep your room neat. You can also give your special projects to grandparents, aunts, uncles and special friends. Our God parents like us to send them our art. Take pictures of your art projects and you won't have to save them all.

Collections

Every kid has a collection. We all like to collect stamps, coins, spoons, cups, etc. To keep your parents off your back and your room neat have a special place for your special stuff. Desk or dresser tops are great places to display your work. Just make sure that your collections are not in the way or will spill out easily. Store them in a secure container. Parents will get annoyed if things are always spilling out. Also, remember the more collections you have the more space you will need. So don't choose a small tight space to store your ever-growing rock collection. Have fun with your collections just don't keep them all over the house.

"Homework is like a little brother, it always wants to spend time with you."

Chapter Four

Everything Has a Place !

Omigosh! Where did you put your school trophy? Nope, not over there. Where are your socks? Ever lose something and get frustrated looking for it. And it seems no one can help you. Well, I'm here to help!

First of all everything has a place and every place has a thing. Well it should have a thing. Now if you want to find your trophy, you gotta clean up and organize. Ready. Let's go!

First things first, if you are going to clean up you need a place to put your stuff. You need a place for absolutely everything. You might try a toy chest or a large plastic storage bin. I like the twenty gallon size my mom gets from Kmart or Wal-Mart. They are usually on sale at back-to-school time

You can also put your favorite things in a storage bin or on display. I know you wouldn't want everything packed away. Neither do I. So perhaps you can put some special things on display and store the other stuff away. Make certain you do it very neatly and do not store things in places where they can easily fall or are hard to get to.

The floor is never a good place to store things. In fact, I'll let you in on a secret when my mom tells me to clean my room, the first place I clean is the floor. When the floor is cluttered with stuff it makes your whole room look junky. So remember the floor is not a place to keep your stuff.

It's easy for me to stay clean now because I have many storage spots for all my stuff. I have a table top which I made out of a storage bin. I put some things inside and store some special things right on the top of the storage bin which I use as a table top. I cover it with a cartoon sheet and it looks nice. I also have a crate, shelf and dresser draws to keep my stuff.

You may not need five places like me to keep all your stuff but I bet you do want some special places to put your things. Try getting your parents to install wall shelves or buying a crate you can put stuff in that you want to keep. Crates are good for toys or items you like carrying from room-to-room

You may also want to put your things in categories before you put them away. It's easy to choose categories just look at the things that usually end up on the floor. Categories are the types of things on your floor. You may need to put all the videos, books, game pieces, etc together. That way it is easier when its playtime, since you can easily locate the toys you want to play with.

Notice the things that keep ending up on the floor. Chances are you do not really have enough space for those things, or else they would not be on the floor. Make a space for them. Use boxes, hang things on the wall. Hooks are great to hold your stuff, although you will need your parents to install them for you. You can also get one of my favorite things the under-bed storage chest. When it's under your bed you can easily slip it out from under the bed.

Force yourself to put things away everyday before you go to bed. Make time daily to clean your room before it looks like a wreck. Make certain everything is put back in its place. Keep a watch on those things that might end up on the floor again even after you have organized.

Try to keep your room clean for a week. Reward yourself for putting things away. When your room gets messy again, write down everything that keeps ending up on the floor. Use the list to help you find new storage spaces. If you keep doing this you just might be able to find your trophy. I hope I helped you.

"It's okay to leave your journal out for your little sister to read as long as she can't read yet."

Chapter Five

Do Your Homework !

Hey, where did your homework go? You started it while you were sitting at the dining room table. Then you heard your little brother laughing at his favorite television show, so you go into the living room to watch.

Then when you came back into the room so your mom could check it,-only it was gone! Your big sister who was setting the table for dinner did not even see a homework book. Sound familiar?

Homework needs to be organized. Schoolwork is our job and we have to learn to do it well. First of all you should have a main working spot for homework. You should have a desk or a specified spot to do your homework.

A homework box with pens, paper, pencils and rulers is really important. If you do not have a desk organizer, you can get a box or a plastic shoebox. I like the plastic ones because you can easily see what is in the containers. Also get in the habit of doing your homework right away so you can have more play-time once you are finished doing your homework. With a VCR you can also record your favorite television shows to watch once you have completed your homework, so don't even think about television.

You also have to force yourself to finish your homework before you do anything else. This is called self-discipline. Tell yourself something like when I'm finished my homework I will have milk and cookies or if I'm done by 6:00 I can watch my favorite show. Keep doing it. It really works. I make special promises to myself and I always keep my word.

There's a secret I have learned about schoolwork. You should never ever say "I can't" to yourself. It's like you stop trying when you say you can't to yourself. Our pastor says words have creative power and I believe him. I get help when I need it but I try to never say "I can't". I just keep trying. You should too! It really is not that hard.

"You can't reach a goal if you don't have a goal. Think about things you really want to do one day and make a goal. You just might reach it!"

Part Two

Time Management
and
Organizing Tips
For
Kids

Time Management
&
Organizing Tips

☺ Even kids need organizers. Ask your mom or dad about getting you an electronic organizer such as a Palm Pilot. You can write down your goals, schedule, homework weekly events, important telephone numbers and your daily activities. See our stuff page for suggested kid items at the end of this book.

☺ Make up some goals. The more goals you have the more you'll accomplish. Of course, don't make too many goals you won't have time to work on them all.

☺ Get up early and have some time by yourself. You can pray, read or just think with no one to bother you. I like just sitting enjoying the quiet.

☺ Make sure you get some relaxed time or quiet time everyday.

☺ Make yourself a morning checklist for you to follow in the morning to help you move faster in the morning. See Worksheet A.

☺ Ask your parents to get you an alarm clock. My grandmother gave me a train alarm clock and it makes a funny train noise at my wake up time. I like it. You can also get a cassette or compact disk alarm clock with your favorite music.

☺ Make a television schedule of the shows you like to watch so you don't watch too much television. Turn the television off as soon as your show goes off.

☺ Decide what you will eat for breakfast at night and put it on the table before you go to bed. You can set the breakfast table for the family at night.

☺ Keep your bags for your activities such as swimming, church, etc. Keep these bags packed and only use them for that activity. Do not use your swimming bag for school, etc.

☺ Make a special bag to take with you when your mom or dad is shopping or keeps you waiting someplace. Put in your bag a notebook, to catch your ideas, drawing paper, favorite books and some small handheld games. You will have something to do while you wait. Keep this bag packed at all times. Trust us you'll need it!

☺ Don't say -"I can't" - because words have power. In our family, we are not allowed to say I can't because when you say I can't you stop trying.

☺ Write out a plan for a perfect day. Most of us plan our days in our heads, but we should get into the practice of writing it down.

☺ Don't try to do everything on your own, ask for help sometimes. For instance, if you do not 100 percent understand how to use the washing machine ask for help. Trust us.

☺ Try to force yourself to do something by treating yourself to something special when you've done a task. Promise you'll read a favorite book while laying on the bed after you clean your room, or maybe you can get can get your favorite snack when you finish your schoolwork.

☺ Put your favorite music in your cassette player and dance while you clean your room or do your chores. It will help you to move faster.

☺ Use the sheets in the back of the book to plan your day. Write out what would be a perfect day. Then write out your actual day activities. Examine both to see where you need to make changes.

☺ Do not let anything distract you when doing your homework including friends, telephone calls and siblings.

☺ Pray for your day. Pray for your teachers, school, family and anyone who will be around you that day.

☺ If you have a big job to do break it down into little pieces. This is especially true of school projects.

☺ Ask your family to get a calendar so you can see what everyone is doing everyday, including you!

☺ Never sit down and watch television. Exercise while you watch your favorite television show. We like to take turns jogging in place or bouncing on our mini-trampoline.

☺ Ask your mom or dad to get you a hanging shoe bag , You can put it on the back of your door or inside your closet to store small items like your cars, small toys and special keepsake items.

☺ When you get a new toy you should give away your old toy. There are lots of kids who are need of good toys that are not broken or damaged. Only give away toys in good condition. Throw old toys away. Giving something to someone who needs it really makes you feel good. Be sure to give away good stuff not junk. Think about how you would feel if you were the other person.

☺ Make zones in your room. A zone is a place where you only do a certain thing. For instance, in my room I have a reading zone and a playing zone.

☺ If your toys don't fit in your toy box or a bin consider giving some toys away or using some of them as display items in your room. For instance, my dolls sit on my bed and dresser.

☺ Ask your mom or dad to buy crates and stack them. They are great to store your toys and books.

☺ Ask your mom or dad to pick a family organizing leader to help keep the house in order. This person will assist your mom or dad in keeping things orderly. It's fun.

☺ When you have to clean a messy room, sort the junk into categories. Start at one place in the room and move around clockwise (the way hands on a clock would move) and do things at each designated clock time. It really works.

☺ Ask your mom or dad to color code your tooth brushes, cups and towels so everyone can be responsible for their own things; also so you don't get blamed for your brother or sister leaving her towel on the floor.

☺ Make your own hygiene box (may use a plastic shoe box) with consists of your own color-coded face towel, cup, tooth brush, hair brush, etc. You can easily remember to do your morning hygiene because everything in the box is sort of a cue. It's hard to forget washing your face when your towel is staring right at you from an open box.

☺ Put all your toys in categories because you usually play with them in categories anyway. You will find it is easier to clean up if you put them all back in one place.

☺ Watch your parents when they do something so you can learn to do it yourself. Also volunteer to help cook the dinner, make the beds, etc so you can really learn for yourself.

☺ When your mom (or dad) tells you clean a room the first thing you should do is clean the floor.

☺ Make the cleaning process go even faster by putting things that go on different floors in your house in a basket by the stairs. When the basket is full someone can take those things upstairs and put them where they belong.

☺ Make a homework box with your school stuff in it. You can put in your pencils, pens, paper, etc.

☺ Break down school projects and home tasks into small easy portions.

☺ Set a deadline before your teacher's or your mom's deadline. Encourage yourself to turn the project in early and make necessary changes. Promise yourself a treat if you finish before the deadline.

☺ Study difficult subjects first especially if you have an exam.

☺ When approaching homework though, do the easy subjects first so that extra time can be spent on the more challenging subjects especially if you need your mom's or dad's help.

☺ Play baroque or classical music to increase concentration when doing hard tasks.

☺ Post a "Quiet-Study Zone" sign on your door.

☺ Try to study in a comfortable place but don't be so relaxed that you fall asleep.

☺ Do not study in bed. Since you sleep in it and associate it with rest it may be difficult for you to concentrate.

☺ Write down words your teacher repeats during a class lecture. She is probably going to put it on the test. This works in Sunday School too!

☺ Lean forward or sit on the edge of your seat when listening to your teacher, mom, dad or your pastor during a sermon.

☺ Read ahead in your textbooks so you can anticipate questions your teacher, dad or mom may ask.

☺ Learn relaxation techniques before an exam. Breathe deeply. Picture yourself doing something fun.

☺ Choose friends who want to excel in school and have similar values and goals. If your good friends do not like a certain friend ask them why. They may have a good reason.

☺ Talk to your friends about your goals. Teach them how to write goals.

☺ Look at your school assignments and chores. Estimate how much time it will take you to complete them. Be honest with yourself. This takes a bit of time. Sometimes we think we can do things faster than we really can do them.

☺ Keep all your books, pens, pencils, etc in one place at home. Set up a study and homework center.

☺ Use Dial-a-Teacher and Tutor programs when you have a question. Most school districts have a Dial-a-teacher program. America On-line has one we use sometimes to help us with questions we have that are not even homework related.

☺ Schedule time with your friends in your organizer.

☺ Let your parents know in advance if you need material for school or an activity. Do not wait until you are writing on the last piece of paper before you tell your parents you need a notebook or the day before a dance recital to tell them your ballet shoes are too tight.

☺ Begin studying for a test as soon as it is announced not the day before the exam.

☺ Get a good night of rest and eat breakfast before exams and strenuous work..

☺ Briefly, look over the entire test before you answer a question.

☺ Answer questions you know first then go back over the ones you do not know on a test.

☺ Study in the early morning not late at night. Studies prove it is better to study in the early morning than late at night.

☺ Exercise regularly. Get involved in an outdoor sport. It will help your ability to concentrate.

☺ Get tutoring early when you realize you are having difficulty with a subject. Be honest with yourself.

☺ Be realistic when you make up your daily "To-Do" list. Think about what you really can do not just what you want to do.

☺ Set goals at the beginning of every week. Also set daily goals. Get your parents input. Let them know when you have major assignments.

☺ Pack your school bag the night before school.

☺ Attempt to become interested in the things you are studying. Relate them to real life or personal goals. This will help improve your concentration

☺ When reading look for the author's point of view. Ask yourself if you agree or disagree.

☺ Know it is okay to disagree with an author's point of view as long as you can state why you disagree with the author.

☺ Pretend you are teaching the material to someone. This will reinforce what you learned. This works with household chores as well.

☺ Do not try to study, if you are too hungry, tired, distracted or not feeling well.

☺ Allow time for information to soak in. Sometimes when learning something new, you need to take a break. Too many new ideas at one time can be confusing.

☺ Avoid procrastination by using parents and friends as accountability partners. Even brothers and sisters can help you keep your word to yourself.

☺ Be sure you understand the homework before you leave school. It is okay to ask questions.

☺ Know it is okay to dislike a subject but you still "have" to do it anyway.

☺ Put reading material at a 45 degree angle so your eyes will be less tired when reading.

☺ Even after you are thoroughly convinced you know a topic engage in over-learning by studying it in a different way, perhaps with a study group or make a game out of the information. You can make up your own flash cards and try to guess the information by turning the card over to see if you are right after saying the information to yourself.

☺ You should always study by yourself first before you study as a group.

☺ Write notes in outline form. It is easier to remember that way.

☺ When reading textbooks turn the chapter and section headings into questions so you can guess what information the author wants you to give you.

☺ Write neatly when taking notes.

☺ Stretch or walk occasionally when you have been concentrating on something for a long time. Home-schoolers should remember to stand and stretch after concentrating for long periods.

☺ Build your concentration by forcing yourself to study a little bit longer each time you study.

☺ When you find yourself daydreaming put a dot on your paper. After awhile you will be able to set a goal to track fewer dots. Reward yourself when you notice you are drawing fewer dots and concentrating more.

☺ Have your parents sign permission slips, report cards, etc at night.

☺ Date all your papers. Put your name on all papers.

☺ Read this book over and over again. You will always find something new you did not quite get the first time.

☺ Think about why you want to do something before you write a goal.

☺ Use your paper/ book organizer and planner before you ask your parents to upgrade you to an electronic organizing tool. Once they see you are faithful with your time using paper they will probably gladly give you the electronic organizer. It is also easier to use the electronic organizer after you have used paper organizers.

☺ You can make your own organizer on the computer. You can use your school or library computer if you do not have a computer. Some computer programs have templates for just making schedule sheets.

☺ Put studying time in your calendar just like you would a football game or a play you want to see.

☺ Study in twenty minute intervals. Stand, Stretch and move when you're studying something.

☺ When your room gets very messy. Take a good look at it. Write down the things you keep finding on the floor (or anywhere it should not be), then write down why you think its there. For instance, if you keep seeing papers on the floor do you need a storage place for your arts and crafts. Talk to your mom or dad about getting storage containers. We like grates and under bed boxes.

☺ If you're reading on your bed make sure you have good lighting or else books will be all over the place because you will tend to read where good lighting exists in your home.

☺ Hanging shoe holders are great if you have limited space. You can hang it on your door or inside your closet door. You can put your small toys or special collectibles in the shoe bag. Explain this to your parents before you ask them to buy the hanging shoe bag. These bags are also pretty cheap so your mom and dad might be willing to try it out.

☺ Limit the zones in your room. We call zones specific places where you do things. We do not eat in our room, nor, do we do arts and crafts in our room. It would be too messy. We only sleep, read and play in our room so it doesn't get too messy.

☺ Always try to get a clear understanding of why your room keeps getting messy. Sometimes our mom and dad would tell us to clean and it would get messy again because we were not really dealing with the problems causing the mess in the first place.

☺ You can tape string from wall-to-wall in your room and hang your art pictures on them.

☺ Label as many things as possible. The labels help remind us where thing s should go. Little kids can also have pictures instead of words on things like dresser draws. You can put a picture of a shirt on your shirt draws.

☺ Organizing does not mean buying stuff. Look around for what you have at home or make things. We use old cereal boxes a lot to make places for our art papers.

☺ When you get a new toy, instead of putting the pieces back into the box which will probably get ripped later, just throw the box away and immediately put the small pieces in a spot where you can easily find them. For instance, when I get a new Barbie™ doll I put the accessories in a Ziploc™ bag and throw out the box right away.

☺ Check off the tips in this book that you want to try out.

"When your parents are talking to good friends at church, just five more minutes really means just five more hours."

Part Three

Questions Kids Ask Us !

Questions

These are questions kids might ask us about organizing. If we do not answer your question in this section, you can email us at kids@momtime.net. Or visit our web page.

Question
My mom is really messy yet she is always telling me to clean my room. I get angry. What should I do?

Answer
Since your mom is also messy maybe you can work together to clean your house. You can find out techniques together and I'm sure this book can help. Maybe you can respectfully ask your mom to read some organizing books. Check out our mom's books. People tell us they like them but if those books don't work keep trying others. The important thing is that you get organized.

Question
When I clean my room my mom and dad tell me it is messy to them. How do I explain to them that it really is clean?

Answer
Maybe room really is messy. Maybe you need to talk to your mom and dad and make a list of what they consider clean. When you do clean your room, use this as a checklist. Perhaps you both can strike a deal as to what is messy and what is not messy.

Question
What do I do? My parents want me to get rid of the car posters on my wall. I love them?

Answer

Point out to your parents as you get older and want to have your own identity that sometimes your room has to be acceptable to you as well as them. As long as it is neat and you do not have anything that is offensive on the wall it is okay. Ask your parents what is the issue they really have with the posters. Do you have too many? Are you ruining the walls? Get the picture? Find out what the real issue is but we agree you should be able to express yourself.

Question

What do I do, my baby brother makes a mess in the house all the time and I have to clean it up?

Answer

Let your little brother watch you and you will become an example with him. You can also tell him that he's your special assistant and let him help you. Little ones like to follow their big brothers so he will probably want to do what you do. Eventually, he will do it himself. Be sure to tell your parents your plan.

Question

What do I do, I share my room with a messy brother?

Answer

If they're little show them how to put back what they take out. You can limit or baby-proof some areas in your room so your little brother cannot get to things. Put things on a high shelf. If they are older, then first have a talk with them telling them how you feel about the room being messy. Remind them a few times. Generally it takes about three weeks or so to form a new habit. It also helps to make room rules and agree on what things you will do in your room. Maybe playing in your room makes it messy. Maybe you can find other places to play. Be sure to read Chapter two in this book on how to live with messy siblings.

Question

My parents don't let me do anything at home. I feel left out. I want to do something. They tell me I'm too young. What should I do?

Answer

You should tell them you feel left out and you want to do more. You can pick a chore you know you can do and suggest it to them. You can also volunteer to help them so you can learn how to do things. See our chore chart to help your parents out a bit.

Question

I keep making a mess out of my room even though I like it clean frequently. I try but I can't seem to be able to keep my room clean. How can I keep my room clean?

Answer

You probably don't have a method to keep it clean. We suggest you figure why and how it gets messy. For instance if you keep finding papers on the floor, do you have a place for your papers? Is the place big enough to store your papers? Are you keeping too many papers? If you are look through them to set which ones are important. Also you should put organizing your room time in your schedule everyday even when your room is clean.

Question

My parents are oh-so-neat, they drive me crazy! They badger me about my room. What can I do?

Answer

Maybe you're not so neat so you drive them crazy too! Or maybe you just need to clean your room a little each day. Talk to your parents and make a contract as to what you both want to see in your room. Explain to your parents you will try to be neat and be yourself at the same time.

Question
I have no room to put anything in my room. What can I do?
Answer
There are several things you can do . First move the things which are not special out of your room. Next, maybe you can hang some things on your wall or your door. Also you might be able to get under-the-bed storage bins which easily slip under your bed. Most important, see if you can throw away or give away anything you may not want anymore.

Question
My mom and dad both work and I am at a babysitter all day, when I get home in the evening I don't have time to clean my room but it seems my room is getting messier and messier. What should I do?
Answer
Maybe, you can wake up early on Saturday mornings and clean your room- that way your whole Saturday doesn't revolve around cleaning your own room. Also you probably need to organize your things because you may be making a mess looking for things and then just leaving the house and not noticing the mess until you get home since you away from home so much.

Question
My mom forgets to sign my notes for school and she gets angry at me when I ask her for money for class trips in the morning. What should I do?
Answer
You should leave forms and reminder notes for your mom in a special place where she can see it. You can put it in the kitchen or living room. You can make a note holder out of an old cereal

box. Simply cut open the side so notes can easily be placed in it. You decorate the cereal box or your mom can buy a Vertical file folder from an Office Supply Store. Remind your mom before you go to bed to look in the box.

Question
I have no time for myself in between piano lessons, little League Practice and the Church youth group. I fell like I have no life of my own. What should I do?

Answer
Maybe you're just doing too much. Ask your parents if you can drop out of some things. Your parents may not understand, when you first approach them. Most likely, you are doing all these things because you wanted to do them and your parents are likely to tell you that! Make a decision to choose just one or two activities to be involved in. Explain to your parents why you want to drop out of an activity. They may not understand at first. Explain to them how you feel stressed for time and think you need to slow time a bit. They tell you need time to think or quiet time. Talk about your feelings. Explain to them you just need a little time for yourself. It might help if you do some of our time worksheets in Part Four first. You can show them how your time is being spent using the worksheets. Sometimes its best to have time for yourself even they would have to agree when they see your time sheets.

Question
I don't have time to practice my trombone yet my parents tell me to find the time. How can I find the time?

Answer
This is a hard question to answer because it depends on your daily schedule. All kids should have studying time, free time and quiet time. Look at your schedule and see how you can change things around. Maybe you can put some practice time into your

free time. Watch also for these time wasters: watching too much television, video games, computer, and talking to friends on the telephone.

Question
My teacher tells me to study for the math test. I do study. I read over all the math problems but then I still do lousy on the test. What am I doing wrong in my study time?

Answer
First, you should put study time in your schedule everyday instead of just waiting until the test comes. Studying is more than just reading over the notes. See our list in the back of books to help kids with their study skills. You can make mock test, outline the material, get old textbooks and form study groups. A great way to study is to pretend you have to teach the material to someone else. This forces you to pay closer attention to the work and catch all the details. If the problem persists, even after trying all of this, then talk to your parents and teacher.

Question
How can I keep things in order in my book bag?

Answer
First, get a bag with at least two or three compartments. This will make it easier to organize your stuff as you put different school supplies in different compartments. If getting a new book bag is not possible then try to make compartments yourself. You can do this by adding your own small bags to your book bag. You can get extra pencil case that remains in your book bag. You can get large cosmetic bags from a novelty store. These bags come in bright solid colors and do not necessarily look like girl bags. Try to carry as few things as possible. Carry with you only the things you really need. Besides it being easier on your back, it will keep your book bag from wearing out. It

takes practice knowing what we really need but if you find you are carrying things from place-to-place without even looking at them then you are carrying too much. You can also make a book bag checklist for yourself to remind yourself what to take and what to leave home or in school.

Question
My desk is a mess? I try to keep it clean but I can't. What should I do?

Answer
Maybe you can put can put a small basket on top of your desk to keep your stuff in. You can also keep a pencil box in or on your desk so you do not have to look for pencils or pens. Remember to put big books on the bottom and small books on the top. You can also put all your workbooks on the left side of the desk and textbooks on the right. If you do not have enough desk space to do this try putting some things on the floor by your feet (the things you do not use very often). You also suggest to your teacher that she gives the class time to organize their stuff. Sometimes you are in such a rush that's why your stuff gets messy. Some kids in traditional school like to use something called deskaroo. It is only $ 6.00 (I think). Check it out at www.deskaroo.com

Question
My parents get mad at me because I forget my books or stuff but I honestly forget them. They punish me I try to remember but still I forget. What should I do?

Answer
You should have a checklist you follow every morning that has everything you need to do so your parents do not have to remind you. You might try having a checklist for school too. Ask your teacher if he can give you, and perhaps the whole class time to go through your checklist.

Question

When its time to leave in the morning. I keep forgetting things in the house. What should I do?

Answer

A checklist always helps us to remember thing. You can post it by the door.

Question

Every Sunday morning we rush, before we go to church. My mom yells at me. She always apologizes later but every Sunday morning it's the same thing! I feel so bad. I don't like getting yelled at and I'm starting not to like church. Can you help me?

Answer

First prepare as many things as possible the night before church. Pick out your clothes, pack your church bag, get your offering and set the breakfast table. Or you can do one thing each weekday night to get you ready for church on Sunday. Also a checklist might also help you and your mom. You might want to guess how much time it takes to do everything to get ready for church. For instance, it may take you twenty minutes in the bathroom but you only plan for ten brief minutes. This causes utter confusion and misunderstanding. Parents call this stress, so make sure you give yourself plenty of time to get ready. See our Church checklist in Worksheet D. Also talk to your mom when she is not rushing and tell her how you feel about her yelling all the time. She might have some good ideas that will help you too!

Question

How can I really manage my time when my parents and teachers are always telling me what to do?

Answer

You can use the planning work sheets to plan the time you can control. You may be surprised at the amount of time you do control. Then once you can see where your time is going and make some goals. See our goal worksheet. Think about the things you really want to do. Put it in your schedule. After you have been following your schedule faithfully , then you will have more credibility with your parents.

Question

I get so overwhelmed with school work and projects. My dad says I start my assignments too late.

Answer

You need to plan out your projects. See our Worksheet J. You need to break your project down into small parts. Also sometimes we need to ask our parents and older brothers and sisters to help us with something. This can be written on your chart. For instance, I cannot go to the library by myself. So, I ask my mom or dad when either of them can take me to the library. I also ask them to put it in their schedule. That's why I like the worksheet. You can put all those things down on your planning sheet. Try it for yourself.

Question

My mom tells me to do things - like the laundry then, gets mad at me when I don't do it right. She doesn't take the time to teach me because she's so busy all the time. What should I do?

Answer

You should talk with your mother and explain you really want to help but you need someone to teach you. There are four steps in learning how to do something. First, you can learn how to do a household chore by watching someone else do it. For instance, watch your mom do the laundry. Second, help her do the laundry. Third ask her to watch you do the laundry. She can correct any mistakes you may be making while she watches you. Fourth, you should only be assigned doing the laundry. Once, both you and your mom know you can do the laundry the right way then you can do it by yourself. Talk to your mom about trying these four steps. It will actually save her time in the long run since she is so busy. If your mom is super busy, older siblings make good teachers too!

Question
My mom and dad give me so many chores I do not have time for myself. What can I do?

Answer
The first thing you should do is talk to your parents. You should tell them how you feel. Perhaps, you can compromise with them. Don't ask to take away too many of your chores at one time. Suggest having certain chores on different days. Creating a family chore list also helps to keep things fair. When you are doing your chores remember to do them quickly and thoroughly then you'll more time to yourself.

Question
My room is messy but I'm so used to messes that I don't even notice it, but my parents are always telling me how messy my room is to them. What should I do?

Answer
You're used to messy, so you have to get used to clean. Clean your room, then ask your parents if they approve of it. Make sure when you clean your room you put things in a place where they can stay so the room can stay clean. Our mom often tells us we have to organize before we can clean. So organize things first. Put things where they belong. Create places for all your stuff. Then clean your room. After your room, has been cleaned and in order for a long while you get used to it being that way and messy will not be normal for you.

Question

I clean my room but then only a few days later, it's a mess again. Papers end up all over the place. What should I do?

Answer

The problem used to happen to us a lot. The real problem is cleaning up your room can be like putting out a fire. You just want to do it quickly especially when your parents are breathing down your back. What we have learned is that if you take the time to figure out why your room keeps getting cluttered. If papers are on the floor don't just throw them in a draw or in the closet, make a specific place for you to put your papers. Make sure the place you put your papers in can really hold all your papers. You also might want to limit the amount of paper you keep. I like to throw old papers out immediately so it doesn't clutter my room. Sometimes I do make a mistake and hold onto papers too long. At those times I know that cleaning my room meaning throwing things out not just putting things away. Remember when cleaning your room throwing things out is just as important as putting things away. When you share a room it's a good idea to agree how much stuff you will accumulate before you start throwing things out.

"It's definitely time to increase your allowance when your dad fires the lawn service and gives you the job"

Part Four

Fun
Charts
and
Checklists

Worksheet A

Suggested AM Checklist

Wake Up

Pray

Make Bed

Get dressed

Brush teeth

Wash your face

Eat breakfast

Worksheet B

Suggested PM Checklist

Straighten up your room

Put on pajamas

Brush teeth

Wash face

Pray

Read

Worksheet C

<u>School Checklist</u>

<u>The Night before</u>
Pack lunch
Pack book bag
Set breakfast table
Have your parents sign all homework, notes and given you trip money if necessary.

<u>The Next Morning</u>
Follow AM Checklist

Listen to the radio. Check the weather to know what kind of covering to wear

Make sure your parents have signed all notes and trip money.

Double-check your school bag one more time.

Worksheet D

Church Checklist

The Night Before

Choose your clothes the night before Church. Get your parents approval for what you want to wear. Iron them or have your parents if necessary. Also choose your shoes and any accessories you want to wear with your church attire.

Get your bible and notebook. Your church bag should always be packed. Be certain to always maintain a separate bag for your church stuff.

Pray for your day

The Next Day
Follow your Am Checklist

Worksheet E-1

Time Chart

Record a perfect day on this chart-how you would like to spend your time

Time	Activity
7:00-7:30	
7:30-8:00	
8:00-8:30	
8:30-9:00	
9:00-3:30	School
3:45-4:00	
4:00-4:15	
4:15-4:30	
4:30-4:45	
4:45-5:00	
5:00-5:15	
5:15-5:30	
5:30-5:45	
5:45-6:00	
6:00-6:15	
6:15-6:30	
6:30-6:45	
6:45-7:00	
7:00-7:15	
7:15-7:30	

Time	
7:30-7:45	
7:45-8:00	
8:00-8:15	
8:15-8:30	
8:30-8:45	
8:45-9:00	
9:00-9:15	
9:15-9:30	
9:30-9:45	
9:45-10:00	**We Suggest You Should be in bed by now**
10:00 - 7:00	**We suggest this should be sleep time**

Worksheet E-2

If you are home-educated here is one made just for you!

Time	Activity
6:15-6:30	
6:30-7:00	
7:00-7:30	
7:30-8:00	
8:00-8:30	
8:30-9:00	
9:00-9:30	
9:30-10:00	
10:00-10:30	
10:30-11:00	
11:00-11:30	
11:30-12:00	
	Continued

	Activity
12:00-12:30	
12:30-1:00	
1:00-1:30	
1:30-2:00	
2:00-2:30	
2:30-3:00	
3:00-3:30	
3:30-4:00	
4:00-4:30	
4:30-5:00	
5:00-5:30	
5:30-6:00	
6:00-6:30	
6:30-7:00	
7:00-7:30	
7:30-8:00	
8:00-	

8:30	
8:30- 9:00	
9:00- 9:30	
9:30- 10:00	**We Suggest you be in bed by now. We are!**

Worksheet F

Time- Record how you actually spent your time. Be honest with yourself!

Time	Activity
7:00-7:30	
7:30-8:00	
8:00-8:30	
8:30-9:00	
9:00-3:30	School
3:45-4:00	
4:00-4:15	
4:15-4:30	
4:30-4:45	
4:45-5:00	
5:00-5:15	
5:15-5:30	

5:30- 5:45	
5:45- 6:00	
6:00- 6:15	
6:15- 6:30	
6:30- 6:45	
6:45- 7:00	
7:00- 7:15	
7:15- 7:30	
7:30- 7:45	
7:45- 8:00	
8:00- 8:15	
8:15- 8:30	
8:30- 8:45	
8:45- 9:00	
9:00- 9:15	
9:15- 9:30	
	Continued on next page
	Continued

9:30-9:45	
9:45-10:00	We Suggest You Should be in bed by now
10:00 7:00	You should be sleeping not recording your time now!

Worksheet G

Write your goals. Remember to put a deadline.
This Example will show you how to do it.

Example

Goal	Deadline
To know my 3 timetables	March 2

Here is a chart to write your goals. A deadline is the time you want to achieve your goal.

Goal	Deadline

Worksheet H-1

Steps To Reach Your Goals

In Worksheet G we made goals, in this appendix you will make steps to reach the goals you wrote. Let's use the example on Work Sheet G.

Example

Goal	Deadline
To know my 3 timetables	March 2-before the math test

Now, write some ways to achieve your goals.
Goal
To know my three timetables

How Do I Achieve This Goal?
I can study more often, I can watch less TV. I can write them on index cards,. I can play my computer math game. I can ask dad to help me.

Worksheet H-2
Sample Goal Worksheet

Goal

_____
_____
_____
_____
_____
_____

How Do I Achieve this Goal?

_____
_____
_____
_____
_____
_____
_____
_____
_____

Worksheet I

Resources

Most of the Organizing resources are for your parents but you can look at the kid stuff and make suggestions to solve your time management and organizing problems.

Website
www.momtime.net/kidscorner
Visit us on the web. Ask questions and give us your suggestions. The only organizing place on the web for parents and kids. Check us out!

Book
500 Ways To Organize Your Child!
This book is good for your parents to read but we think you might enjoy it too. We helped our mom write this book. It was fun. You will find lots of practical information. It's a great book to read with your parents.

Parents also may like some of our mom's other books including Put Your Home in Order and Put Your Life in Order.

These websites are mainly for adults. We think we are the only Kid Professional Organizers we know. Still we thought you might want to look at their websites. They do have stuff for kids.

Online Organizing has great parent Organizing Packages. They also have stuff for kids too! You will find hooks, storage, etc. just for kids. Your parents will really like this website. Check them out at www.onlineorganizing.com

The Organized Student is a great website. Check it out at www.organizedstudent.com. Your parents can get a list of school supplies to help you be more organized.

Check out the www.newhomemaker.com. Your parents will find things to help you get organized.

Check out www.overhall.com/kids. Your parents will find this site useful.

Check out this website www.organizedhome.com

Check out www.faithfulorganizers.com

Worksheet J

Study Planning Sheet Sample

Preparation Time	Resource	Estimated Time	Other
Monday 4:15 PM	*Library books*	*2 hours*	Ask dad to drive me
		Total Time	

Worksheet K

<u>Daily To Do Chart</u>

✎ List activities and assign a numerical value

A- Most important-Must do!

B- Should Do-Have to do!

C- Could do-May do it

A B or C	Time	Activity	Estimated Time To Complete
A	7:00	Finish Math Homework	45 Min

Worksheet L
Fun Family Checklist

Did hug everyone today?

Did I say an encouraging word today?

Did I help someone without being asked to do so?

Did I talk to God today?

Did I practice self-control today?

Did I play without bickering today?

Did I help mom and dad today?

Did I do my chores today?

Did I do my homework neatly today?

Worksheet M

Chores For Different Ages

2 years - 6 years

Pick up their toys

Sort silverware

Put their clothes in labeled dresser drawers

Help sort laundry

Wipe down dinner / breakfast table

Wipe base boards

Pull up covers on their crib / toddler bed

Help load the dishwasher

Set the table

Weed the yard

Water plants

Use non-toxic spray cleaner in the bathroom & kitchen

Daily use disinfectant wipes in the bathroom

Empty wastebaskets

Use a handheld vacuum cleaner

Assist mommy and daddy with chores

7 years -12 years

The entire chore list of 2yr-6yr and:

Wash and dry dishes

Rake leaves

Assist snow shoveling

Unload dishwasher

Damp mop floors

Vacuum floors

Care for pets

Make simple microwave meals

Wipe counters

Wipe down walls using non-toxic cleanser

Clean outdoor furniture

Assist in preparing family meals

Make your own beds

Clean your own rooms

Organize your toys

Take telephone messages

Do household filing

Assist in mowing the lawn

Dust furniture

Make shopping list

Put away groceries

Weed garden

Plant flowers in the yard

Wash siding

Make their own lunches

Wash the car

Help care for family pet

Sort mail

Organize family cassette tapes,

Organize compact disks

Organize videocassette tapes

Clean windowsills

Water lawn

Take out garbage

13 years – 18 years

The entire chore list for 7yr-12 yr and:

Prepare family meals

Go grocery shopping

Scrub the bathroom

Wax floors

Mow the lawn

Use the trimmer and cut hedges

Care for younger siblings

Clean the garage

Tutor siblings

Take care of family pet

Organize family files

Organize family library / books

Work as a secretary or receptionist in family home business

Wash blinds

Clean out refrigerator

Do their own laundry

Train younger siblings in household tasks

Polish furniture

Help plan the family budget

Chauffeur younger siblings to activities

Run errands for family

Study Tips For kids

Picture the directions in your mind. Form a visual picture after your teacher gives you instructions. Imagine a circle when the directions are Circle the correct answer.

Sit in the front of the class if possible. It is easier to pay attention. Also the teacher can see your facial expressions and may further explain a point.

Watch your teacher's nonverbal cues. Notice their facial expression and mood changes.

Watch what excites your teacher about the lesson. This is likely to be on the exam.

When you are listening intently, lean forward to the edge of your seat.

Assume the teacher will only give the instructions once. Do not anticipate that the teacher will repeat himself.

Review your notes before class.

Ask the teacher a question concerning the assignment. Think of a question. This forces the teacher to interact with you and demonstrates that you will want to learn.

Remember there is no such thing as a dumb question. When in doubt, ask.

When forming study groups do not look to friends but to others who have good work or study ethics.

Take a lot of notes but condense them after class into a smaller organized outline.

You should study everyday even if you do not have homework.

Put your studying time in your calendar. Treat these times like appointments that must be kept.

Look at your assignments and estimate how much time it will take you to complete it.

When learning a foreign language you can get language audio tapes from most public libraries.

Congratulations !

You have just completed a Kid's Guide to Organizing. We hope these skills will help you as you grow. It has helped us. We had fun writing it and we hope you had fun reading it. Write to us and let us know how you liked this book or to share your organizing tips for a future edition of this book.

Write us at
Jehonadah Communications
P.O. Box 712
Long Island, New York 11553-0712

Visit our website www.momtime.net
Click Kids Corner to email us

About The Authors

Jarrett G. Carter is 11 years old. His hobbies are drawing, reading and writing. Jarrett says it wasn't easy for him to switch from being messy to being organized back when he was just eight. He hopes this book will make it easier for you. He says he has had experience with being messy and organized. He prefers being organized. He is sure you will too!

Janae J. Carter is 8 years old. Her hobbies are drawing, dancing, reading and writing. She really likes schoolwork. Janae says writing this book helped her to become more organized herself. She confesses she is still working on her organizing skills. She encourages you to keep working at it too!

Jolene T. Carter is 5 years old. Her hobbies are playing all sports, writing and reading. Jolene says that she is still working on becoming organized but she is in no rush to learn.

Jarrett Carter, Janae Carter, and Jolene Carter are all home educated students. They play the recorder and are active in their church, community and home school group. In addition, to being freelance writers, they assist their mom in her company Organize Your Life! They helped her write 500 Ways to Organize Your Child, a book for parents.

Their friend Brandon Locke inspired them to write this book after he told them there were no organizing books for kids. The Carter kids agreed with him. They decided to write their own book because as they theorize" now-a-days adult books are too complicated for kids and kids need to be organized too!"

An Important Note

We hope you learned something and enjoyed reading this A Kid's Guide To Organizing. You can visit our web page at

www.momtime.net/kidscorner.html

We will answer kids' questions about organizing. Our mom and dad check out mail so kids only please. Please remember, we <u>only</u> answer questions related to organizing. We look forward to hearing from you. You can also send us your organizing and time management tips and read our monthly newsletters (on organizing of course!)

Contact them (kids only please) at: kids@momtime.net

Or visit their website at:
www.momtime.net/kidscorner

Parents may contact our mom at:
Cheryl@momtime.net

Write to us at:
Carter Kids
c/o Jehonadah Communications
Post Office Box 712
Long Island, New York 11553-0712

500

Ways
to Organize Your
Child!

By Cheryl R. Carter

This book has over 500 ways parents can help their children become more organized. It also contains parental principles and questions parents ask about organizing and time management. Get it at local bookstore or online at Amazon. Com, Barnes and Noble.com or Borders.com or visit our website at www.momtime.net

Only $ 11.95 !

Volume discounts available for Educators, schools, organizations, churches and groups.

Check out our other books.

Visit our website
www.momtime.net

Put Your Home In Order!
A Practical Guide for Bringing Peace& Order to Your Home.
Cheryl R. Carter 12.95

Put Your Life In Order!
A Simple Guide To Time Management, Goal Setting and Productivity Just For Women-2nd Edition
Cheryl R. Carter 14.95

500 Ways To Organize Your Child!
Cheryl R. Carter 11.95

God and Time
Beyond Time Management to a God-Directed Life- $15.95
Cheryl R. Carter

NOTES

CPSIA information can be obtained at www.ICGtesting.com
Printed in the USA
BVOW071243170413

318392BV00003B/1039/A